Flip the Flaps

Animal Homes

Judy Allen and Simon Mendez

Schools Library and Information Services

KINGFISHER

First published 2009 by Kingfisher
This edition published 2012 by Kingfisher
an imprint of Macmillan Children's Books
a division of Macmillan Publishers Limited
20 New Wharf Road, London N1 9RR
Basingstoke and Oxford
Associated companies throughout the world
www.panmacmillan.com

Consultant: David Burnie

ISBN 978-0-7534-3638-7

1 3 5 7 9 8 6 4 2
1TR/0912/UTD/LFA/157MA

A CIP catalogue record for this book is available from the British Library.

Printed in China

Contents

Trees

A tree is a bit like a block of flats, with homes at every level. Birds and squirrels nest in the branches. Small animals live in cracks in the bark. Woodpeckers may live in a hole in the trunk.

squirrel

thrush nest

1. Do the small animals
ever come out from
under the stones?

2. Why isn't there a
spider in that web?

3. Do worms live
under stones?

ladybird

1. Yes. The animals come out to eat. Most eat leaves and soggy wood.

2. The spider hides with one foot on the web. A trapped insect will move the web and the spider will pounce.

3. Worms live in the earth. But if a stone is on top of earth, there might be worms underneath.

earwig

ladybird flying

centipede

worm

millipede

springtail

Burrows

A fox's home is called an earth or den. It is a burrow where the female fox has her cubs. She does not make a nest, so the cubs all sleep on the bare ground. Adult foxes mostly sleep outside.

fox cubs playing

8

1. Do all foxes live in burrows?

2. Are foxes good at digging burrows?

3. Do other animals live in burrows?

1. Do frogs spend all
   their lives in ponds?

2. Why are dragonfly
   young under the water?

3. Can pond animals live
   underwater all the time?

froglet

frog

1. No. Tadpoles hatch from frogspawn, become froglets and climb out. Adult frogs live on land and in ponds.

2. Dragonflies lay their eggs on pond plants underwater. The young hatch and live in the pond for two years.

3. Some can. Others, like the diving beetle, take an air bubble down with them.

dragonfly young

A dragonfly young changes

A dragonfly!

crawling out of old skin

young crawling out of pond

11

Shells

Animals with shells already have homes. Some can go inside their shells and sleep safely. Only the hermit crab doesn't grow its own shell. It finds an empty one to move into.

hermit crab

Lobsters and mussels also have shells.

1. Why are the shells empty?

2. Where do hermit crabs find the empty shells?

3. Do turtles change their shells when they need bigger ones?

turtle

1. When an animal with a shell dies, its body shrivels up and an empty shell is left.

2. A hermit crab finds empty shells on the sea floor. As the crab grows, it has to find a larger shell.

3. No. Like snails, their shells are part of their bodies and grow bigger with them.

hermit crab moving into a new shell

A snail's shell grows with it

Young snails have small, soft shells.

The shell grows bigger and harder.

Caves

There are sea caves, ice caves and land caves where bats may live. Some bats sleep in cracks, while others sleep upside down.

bat

1. When do bats sleep?

2. Is it cold in a cave?

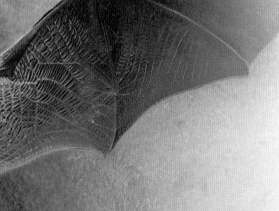

3. What else lives
in a bat cave?

bats getting
ready to sleep

1. Bats sleep by day. At night, they fly out to feed.

2. Yes, it may be cold in a cave, but it is sheltered from winter wind and rain.

3. Lots of insects, and spiders and scorpions, too. They are often white if they always live in the dark.

Other animals in a bat cave

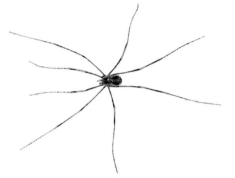

harvestman

cockroach

cave cricket

cave beetle

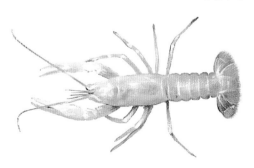

cave crayfish

15

Home-builders

Beavers use branches and stones to build a lodge in a river or lake. They can bite right through trees with their sharp teeth and chew the wood into useful lengths.

beaver lodge

16

1. Where is the entrance to the beaver lodge?

2. Do beavers eat fish?

3. Do other animals build homes?

1. The lodge entrance is underwater.

2. No. Beavers eat plants, twigs and tree bark. They store food in the water around the lodge or in a room inside it.

3. Yes. Birds, squirrels and bees all build homes. The tailorbird makes a home by sewing leaves together.

A tailorbird builds a nest

sewing together leaf edges

safe in the nest

17

Index